To: Aleriah

REVELATIONS OF AN
UGLY OLD HAG

a true &
Wonderful
friend

Dolly D

REVELATIONS OF AN UGLY OLD HAG

DOLLY DELANTY

Library of Congress Control Number: 2016913260
ISBN: Hardcover   978-1-5245-3278-9
                 Softcover   978-1-5245-3277-2
                 eBook   978-1-5245-3276-5

To order additional copies of this book, contact:
Xlibris
1-888-795-4274
www.Xlibris.com
Orders@Xlibris.com
741979

CONTENTS

PREFACE

I am a senior who has written the following essays in parody form. It is hoped that no offense is made on any personal level. If a reader thinks something pertains to him, I am truly sorry. All of us have idiosyncrasies, which could match something they read in my book. That is what makes us—as human beings—interesting and separates us as individuals. Any similarities to persons or places or things are purely coincidental.

I hope you will read my essays and enjoy them as much as I did in writing them.

Dolly Delanty
2016

INTRODUCTION

I have written a book about different stories describing, in my own way, what I go through when I go down to visit my daughter and family in Australia and also of my life before and after I went to a retirement home, which I call the Gulag. It's somewhere in Canada. After you read my essays, you will understand why I prefer to not specify where the locality of my retirement residence is.

I tend to jump around as far as the topics of my essays are concerned. It is hoped that you realize that they are all written "tongue-in-cheek" and in my own "crass" way.

I don't like the men Down Under, and I feel the same way about the women... Australians might not like this when they read the book.My oldest daughter lives there, so I stay with her and her husband on their estate, which is near a rain forest. In Southern Australia. ` I'm sure Jack, my son law is glad when the old bitch (meaning me) goes home. Mind you, he's always great to me. It's what he says when I'm not there. I'll never be welcome there after he reads this book! Probably immigration will be sure to flag me when they see me as well.

The first time I visited Australia, I got the fucking orientation shit from my daughter. She said, "Mom! There're some things you just don't say. Like, men are easily offended here."

Poor babies! It's like "When you cross *me*, you bitch, you are crossing *all* the rest of the men in Australia." What a bunch of crap. The Aussies were supposed to be the toughest fighting men during World War II. What happened to them, anyway?

I bloody hope you will also enjoy my stories of my life in my retirement home. The experience of moving to the Gulag was a fucker of an adjustment for this ugly old hag!

Come on, people. I put my body and soul into these essays!

Read on.

MORE ABOUT ME AFTER MOVING INTO THE "GULAG"

I like reading. Hell, I read an average of eight to nine books a week, so I feel I am an expert on lots of things. That includes the social sciences . . . like sex. After reading what I am writing, the "purple brigade" at my new home are bound to turn on me.

"She's gone rogue . . . crazy. She's no longer one of us. Let's boycott her book!"

Go right ahead.

Shit, I know I have je ne sais quoi. It's undeniable. This ugly old hag is having a ball. Who says life ends at eighty? I'm so excited—and not from my vibrator. By the way, I was sure to include that little toy when I knew I was moving into the home, or Gulag as I call it. One time, my doctor asked me if I was still sexually active. I answered, "Of course I am."

At that time, I was dating a guy who was thirty-five years younger than me. There was a drawback though. He couldn't "get it up." It wasn't too long before I found out he had a foot fetish. He spent a lot of time licking my feet and toes. The fact that he was filthy rich helped things though, and the diamonds were great. He told me he wasn't married, but I kinda doubted it. After I gave him the boot, his real wife called me an ugly old hag on Facebook, hence the name of my book. I thought it was rather catchy.

Tile Rummy and bingo really catch hell around the Gulag. Are *you* "feeling it"? I bet you can hardly wait to join me.

The staff has been super educated to know how to deal with us around here—to recognize our needs, so to speak. Well, how about anger management classes for us Gulagers?

"Shit, here he comes." Our newspaper bandit. The asshole can't wait to grab the newspaper first thing in the morning. Even worse—how about the dickhead who reaches over and grabs the best big, fat, juicy grapes off the plate in the morning?

My youngest daughter came yesterday to take me out for Mother's Day. I called her over to my computer and said, "I want you to read this. Please be open-minded." Well, it went the way I thought it would . . . bloody bad. Exclamations like "Ewwwwwww . . . oooh . . . shit, Mom, you can't write that. Please say you aren't going to say that?"

I even heard expletives that I have never heard before. Well, she started to talk to me eventually. I did remove *cunnilingus* out of the above to make her feel a little better.

PS: My ob-gyn doctor told me that the incidence of STDs is extremely big in retirement and nursing homes. What do you think of that? Looking around me, I don't know how any of the men can do anything vaguely resembling the sex act. Bloody hell! Most of them are in their eighties and nineties. It looks to me that the ladies could be up for it though. Hooray for woman power!

BEAUTY SALON DAY

Today's the day for my hair and eyebrow care. We have our own beauty salon. Sometimes I don't think they know what they're doing. I end up with a fucking ugly haircut. I told 'em that I didn't want a damn "old lady" cut. It doesn't seem to matter. I looked like halfway between a beaver and a hedgehog.

One time, I told them to branch out and try something new. When I walked out, my fucking hair was half an inch long. You'd think I was having chemotherapy! A lot of the old bats come and have a permanent. Who bloody well has one these days? I don't think the beauty operators even know how to give one anymore. If they do, it looks like they have a Brillo pad sitting on their head.

I am due to have my eyebrows waxed and dyed. I look like Groucho Marx without the mustache. They just can't get it right. The next thing you know, I'll be sporting a bloody unibrow. I've given up.

I get them to tweeze the hairs on my chin at the same time. I was told by a doctor that the reason us old ladies have hair on the face is because we're not getting sex anymore. It has to do with not having any damn orgasms, which gets rid of the nasty ole male hormones. I fucking believe it. I'm too tired to test the theory though. It's easier to pay for tweezing, but it's not as much fun.

I asked them if they do full Amazons. They looked at me as if they didn't hear right.

"Amazon? You don't mean . . . Brazilian"—big gulp—"wax?"

I said, "Oh sorry, yep, that's what I meant."

They told me they don't do them, but they could give me the name of a place that does.

BINGO NIGHT

Thought I would have a gambling night. As I walked to the activity room, I could hear the high, shrieky voice of Estelle. Christ! Don't tell me *she's* calling again? Yep! She speaks like Elmer Fudd.

"Dolly, would you pweeze sit in the chair beside Wachel?" she squeaked.

Because I got there late, all the damn cards were picked over. They were fucking crappy.

High stakes tonight. Cost me all three dollars. Estelle got a new set of balls. They were blue!

Shit, I didn't like 'em. The other ones were white. Kinda put me off. Everyone else loved 'em.

She got a new basket for her bloody new balls as well. She started to call, and it happened. A ball flew out of the basket and nailed Harold right on his farting forehead!

I'm glad because I couldn't stand the little bastard. He lives down the hall from me. He used to leave his door open all the time, for me. For a while, he used to leave me a wilted flower he got from the tables at my doorstep. He talks dirty, you know. I think he has sex on his mind all the time. He's ninety! He probably wanted to cop a feel.

Anyways, poor Harold had to leave bingo because he was getting a bump on his forehead as big as an egg. I heard he called the desk to have the nurse come up and put some ice on it. I wondered if he tried to cop a bloody feel. Probably.

There was a lady who really didn't know where she was most of time, who kept calling "bingo." Now that's bloody annoying for us hard-core gamblers. It took us two hours to play four games! I'm not going again.

This is not as fun as casino night.

BOOZE

I used to drink in my early years. Wouldn't drink hard stuff. Didn't like the damn taste. Corona was what I liked. Hell, I could drink truck drivers under the bloody table.

When I was married the first time, my husband loved to take me to the beer parlors and make money on me. No, he didn't pimp me out! He would say, "Hey, you guys, wanna see my wife chug-a-lug?"

The bastards would all say "sure, sure" and laugh. Here's this example of the "inferior race," obedient wifey—who, by the way, should be home with her kids instead of sitting there with *them* at *their* table—and her shit of a husband (who, I found out too late, was boinking other women) said she could beat *them* at drinking?

T̶h̶... ...did they know that I could beat any

...s the way it was. Man, the shit really hit the fan with my first husband. I divorced the bastard after ten years of hell. The things I found out about him. Example: I used to wonder why he took so long to take the babysitter home. He was screwing my best friend at the CNR yards while I was waiting for him.

Well, to make a long story short, my drinking came to an end a few years down the line—after husband no. 2. I think. I had been imbibing red wine with a close girlfriend of mine in another town.

She said, "You can stay here tonight."

I slurred, "No, I gotta go home, right now. Right now, if not sooner."

I proceeded to drive home, but I was having some trouble focusing. Somehow, I lost my bloody way, and about two blocks away from my house, I got caught up on some guy's retaining wall. The bloke came out and said, very kindly, "Here, I'll drive you home, lady."

The next day, there was a fucking knock at the door.

The police! They're after me.

I opened the door, and someone shoved part of my tailpipe at me.

"Here, I think this belongs to you," the young man said.

"Don't feel bad. I've been there too," he said.

Haven't drunk since, but sometimes I would like a nice Corona on a hot day.

PS: I was a bad girl.

BORSCHT NIGHT

I make the best damned borscht[1] in the world. Trouble is that I only have a pissy two burner stove at my place. So I decided to take it to another level and use our public kitchen to make it. It didn't take long for word to get around the home. Suddenly there was a large crowd rubbernecking.

I make the Doukhobor borscht. I knew someone whose mother-in-law was a Doukhobor, and that's where I got the recipe. There're at least six steps to achieve the damn soup. It's worth it!

I am the worst, messiest cook in the world. Working with beets can be a problem. First, you have to boil the bone, then throw a potato into the broth, and then sauté beets, cabbage, and tomatoes and throw them into the mix. Then dice some more beets, shred more cabbage, and dice carrots and potatoes, and then add, simmer then, when partially cooked, add fresh dill weed and cream. Then add more shredded cabbage. Let it sit.[2] The recipe is at the back of this book.

By this time, I have all the damn pots and pans dirty, and I'm fucking splattered with beet juice and tomatoes. The whole bloody lot wanted to have some, but none of them offered to help clean up! The asses! I felt like kicking them down the hall, walkers and all.

---

[1]   I'm not making it again. The recipe for the borscht is at the back of this book.

[2]   See appendix

Chef heard about my borscht and came running. The bastard said he thought it lacked something after he tasted it. Needless to say, Claude (pronounced *Clode*) had two bloody bowls of it. He refused my recipe. Said he had his own. It tastes like shit.

MORNING BREAKFAST AT THE GULAG

What a fuck up! I went down the first few mornings I was here and that was enough. All those bags do is talk about their bowels and their doctor's visits. Well, I guess there isn't anything more to talk about, other than yapping about their problems and getting the latest shit on so-and-so.

The early bird gets the worm, but you gotta get there first. There's always some idiot that grabs the best bananas and the juiciest grapes. If you're late getting there, all the good fruit is picked over too. The walker brigade is out in full force, so you're bound to get a poke in the bloody shin from someone pushing their farting walker right into you. It's a regular free-for-all. Some of the residents raid the food bar, grab everything in sight, and throw the damn stuff into their catchall compartment of their walker. Balls! They must be feeding their whole damn family with it.

The other day I heard the kitchen ran out of oatmeal porridge. My god, *that* was awful! Some son of a bitch swung his cane and whacked a fellow Gulager on the knuckles for taking the last of the porridge. Kinda hitting below the belt when one of mine is on the receiving end.

I guess you can see it's the survival of the bloody fittest around the Gulag.

BRIDGE

Some of my Gulager friends and I decided to play some bridge. That was a bad farting choice! It didn't take long to find out that we didn't belong there. Hey, that didn't stop us. We're relentless. Luckily, I knew the rules. Used to play with my dad. He was a terrible role model. He used to open with bidding three hearts, and he only had five points! I think he was crazy.

Anyways, we were instructed by the big kahuna to sit down at these stupid little card tables. Jeez! I thought they went out with the horse and buggy.

Just then an old bugger shuffled in and said, "For Christ's sake, don't sit me with Anita." I felt sorry for him because Anita was a dizzy dame who didn't know her ass from a hole in the ground.

"I'm sorry, Ernest, but you know that requests like that are not allowed," the big kahuna said.

He said, "But I can't stand the bitch."

I should give you the back story. Anita is crazy about Ernest. She haunts that poor little guy. Wants to sit with him on the bus, and always makes a beeline for a seat next to him in the dining room. Jeez! She obviously wants to get into Ernest's pants. Well, Ernest left in a big hurry, and Anita had to make do.

I was seated opposite a stuffy old Brit called Mona. She always looked like she could smell something bad.

She said, "I say, do you play bridge often?"

I answered, "Hell, yeah."

"Jolly good," she said, with little conviction.

Anyways, I'm not going into the messy details. They managed to kick me and my fellow Gulagers out. Bloody hell. They said we were disruptive, of all things.

BUDGIE EPISODE

Budgies are big in Australia. Jack had a huge ten-foot high budgie house he built himself. He must have had at least twenty birds chirping away in the damn thing. And did he love his budgies! I can remember him walking the property, admiring his birds with his "budgie smuggler" (Speedo) on. Shit, that was something to see!

Anyways, back to the story. I'm sorry. I get caught up in other things. Especially when Jack, my son-in-law, is concerned. He had a dog named Sweetie, and she used to drive his birds crazy. They were forever pulling their tail feathers out because the stupid dog scared the shit out of them by circling around their cage. Sweetie was a purebred border collie and felt like she was herding sheep, I guess. The poor little birds were basically a nervous wreck. I don't see the connection, but then, I'm not Sweetie.

One time some ass had left the cage door ajar, and away they went. They never came back. Poor Jack had to replace every one of his budgies, again. I think he should have gotten rid of the dog instead.

Now, Jack had a very large tin, which he kept in the kitchen. He kept his supply of birdseed in it. My daughter and I used to keep contact by phoning, and as a result, her phone bill escalated to hundreds of dollars. She was careful to watch when the phone bill came so she could intercept it . . . sneaky what? She would peruse it and then bury it in the seed can—thinking that, of course, she would retrieve the bill and pay it another day, which bloody well never happened.

Sometime down the line, Jack would have to top up the birds' fucking seed, so the asshole would lumber to the tin and scoop some seed up. Unfortunately, my daughter had not buried the last bill well enough. And up it came.

Can I say the shit hit the fan that day? Yeah, it sure did. I was in the pool at the back, but I heard the thunder coming from the kitchen. When my daughter came home from work, he let her have it. She just stood there and laughed at the fucking idiot. She was loving every minute of it. You'd be surprised how many wives threaten their husbands with kitchen knives!

Well, "ya gotta do what ya gotta do," which, by the way, is one of my most favorite sayings.

THE CHAT ROOM

I thought it was time that this ugly old hag tried a chat room experience. The only trouble is that you end up glued to your fucking computer for hours at a time. So, if you are going to do it, you'd better make it worth your while.

The next thing I knew . . . I was in love! His name was Bo. He's from North Carolina. He told me that he was a representative for his County. I think he's Democratic. Hell, I'm a Canuck. I don't know shit about the USA!

I asked him if he was married. He said yes, but his wife doesn't like the public arena life. So she lets him do his thing. Sounds damn fishy to me. He has an apartment near the state legislature. He sent me a picture of him meeting and greeting his constituents. He's kinda cute but a little long in the teeth. Seventy-seven years old. I like 'em around sixty or so. There's nothing like a younger guy though. It sure puts the pep in the old hag's step.

I got kinda tired of him 'cause he bloody didn't want to expand our relationship and take it to another level." The nerve of the old creep!

This all happened about ten years ago. So I got on the Internet the other day and googled the bastard. Bo is still going strong. Good for Bo. Obviously, his stents are holding up.

CLEANING MARMIE'S CAT BOX

I love my cat. But I have to make sure she has a clean facility like me. I have it under the sink in the bathroom. I've got no other place for it. I know it's bloody gross. I use little pellets of recycled paper for the litter. I'm very ecology minded. The only drawback is after she does her business, she jumps out and flicks the shitting little pellets all over the bathroom floor. I always have to shake my shoes out before I put them on. Those bloody little pellets really hurt.

Well, Marmie always decides to do her dump at three thirty every morning. The rank smell wakes me up out of a sound sleep. And she is so damned proud of herself and excited at what she's done that she goes crazy, racing all over the apartment. What is there about having a dump that excites her so much? I know *I* bloody don't get excited when I do. Maybe relieved, but not crazy excited!

So I have to clean the fucking cat box before I go back to sleep. Then I have to take the baggie down to the garbage room after sticking my head out to make sure there is no one around. They don't like us walking around in our kimono. I take my chances.

I buy fifty-pound bags at a time. It's damn good that I've got one of those fancy-shmancy buggies all the old ladies pull behind them. Mine is black and white polka dots.

Marmie used to be upchucking fur balls all the time, so now I buy really expensive food for her so she passes the balls. Listen, my cat gets the royal treatment. I give her glucosamine for her little joints as well. She's a fucking princess around here!

DO I LIKE IT HERE AT THE GULAG?

It's been eight long months down the line. I'm still here. They say you can get used to anything. I'm bloody well getting to like the place . . . kinda. It's hard for me to toe the line sometimes though. For a girl with my sensibilities, it's been a real stretch. I haven't had too much trouble with the staff, which kind of surprises me. They seem to enjoy me. That's too bad because I sure as hell don't enjoy them one bit.

My favorite mantra is "what am I doing here?" I'm here because my miserable daughters sent me to a retirement home, that's why! They dumped me and buggered off. Maybe I may change my will.

I'm slowly turning the tide here. There are more Gulagers. Haven't reached the men yet.

Don't worry, it's bound to happen. I feel I am a force now.

Just as an aside, which doesn't have anything to do with what I'm yakking about, I had a dream last night where a samurai warrior has kidnapped me. He and I are galloping along on his white steed.

How about this one? It was in France, and I was kneeling at the guillotine waiting for the damn blade to fall. I think I must have been Anne Boleyn or something. I should go to a shrink and find out.

Both my daughters' marriages broke up. I spend a lot of time Skyping with the one in Australia. Jack, her husband was always cool to me but left a lot to be desired as a husband. Those Aussie men. They're all the same fucking asses. They're all ugly anyway just like British guys.

Have you noticed that the Brits have large noses just like the French? I notice things like that! Hey, I'm not saying it. You know what I mean. You thought I would, didn't you?

Anyways,'Im s'posed to be talking about myself, which I love. I gotta admit that this place is growing on me. I spend a lot of time watching Netflix in our theater. I used to act. Didn't go far but did appear in a friend's movie. I was the grandmother who fell down the stairs, some asshole pushed me. They had a stunt guy take the fall. I offered to do it, but they said no.

Below is an example of a busy day for us Gulagers:

    9:30—morning walk
    10:15—test your marbles
    1:30—afternoon bridge
    1:30—hand chimes
    2:30—choir practice
    6:30—big bingo

As you can see, they keep us busy.

DOCTOR'S VISIT

I hate going to the farting doctor. I think I am the only Gulager who avoids going. Everyone else around here just loves talking about their last damn visit. It is the highlight of the week for them. Not me!

When I moved here, I had to find a private doctor that's within walking distance. I got one! Never mind that his receptionist can't speak a damn word of English. That's okay because he does speak the bloody language and is a living doll. The minute he walked in with my chart I thought, *I've hit the mother lode.* Tall, dark, and handsome.

I thought I had better read him the riot act. "I don't want a mammogram. I don't want to see you except to reorder my pills or if I'm dying. I don't want to give a stool specimen and no bloody pelvics."

He looked at me for a minute and then said "okay."

I found out, when I was a nurse, that the doctors who were "nicey nicey" were usually the worst. The ones who were miserable buggers were the best. In other words, beware of those who are fucking Mr. Congeniality. It's not unheard of for these nice guys to cop a feel once in a while.

THE DRAMA CLASS AT THE GULAG

Decided to start a drama club. I'm a little bit of a dramaturge myself. Have written and produced before I came. I know you're thinking, *Is there anything this woman can't do?* Not damn much! I'm fucking multifaceted. You name it, I've done it.

Well, it was a bloody disaster, that's what it was. Shoulda' known. It's like talking to a bunch of breathing (barely in some instances), eating, pooping robots. There were six people there. Oh, the little guy who intoned the Lion and the Mouse in the shuttle bus was there. I knew he would be there for sure.

You gotta have control of the group, I knew that. Didn't fucking help. There was a real nice lady who was there but didn't know why. That's dumb. There was a gal who thought it sounded interesting. Then how about the jerk who was well on the way to being pissed? Well, you never know. John Barrymore Jr. was always three sheets to the wind and gave his best performances. The other two? Might as well forget them.

I thought we would start with improvisation because no one can even vaguely remember their names, never mind dialogue, and I thought knowing how to improvise would help them onstage if they fumble their farting lines.

The Thespian starts with, "This party is great. I'm having such fun. Oh no, she's coming over here."

The Jerk pipes up with, "How do you like this?" And she starts doing the pelvic thrust. I forgot to mention that the Thespian was stone-blind.

He says "what are you doing?" in the direction of the Jerk who is knocking back a full glass of red wine while gyrating.

The rather nice lady seems to want to enter the damn fun and says, "Uh . . . uh . . . uh, well . . . she's doing . . . what's that called?" to whoever can answer. One of the two remaining says "Well, she's dancing for you" to the Thespian.

The Thespian, who is very British and is ninety something, says, "How perfectly kind of you."

I could see that this little exercise was not working. I could read the writing on the wall. Shit! This whole thing was not going to work.

So that was the end of that!

ELLEN

One of my best friends is a tranny. She is wonderful. I bloody love traveling in her circles. It's just another facet of my life, knowing her.

One day she asked me if I could write her biography, and I jumped at the request. Hell, I can write about anything. It would be a damn best seller. For some reason, her lawyer wouldn't allow it.

I don't think the people in the Gulag even know the slightest thing about the tranny life. One day I tried to take a blue-hair aside and enlighten her. She just looked at me and clicked her bloody tongue. What in the hell is that supposed to mean?

Yesterday, I was waiting for Ellen to pick me up. She was going to take me out for lunch. She pulled up in a late-model cobalt-blue convertible Mustang! I was glad that there were a lot of people there. You should have seen their faces! They all wanted to know who she was.

Ellen bounded out of her car and came in and gave me a huge hug. She was built like a bloody Amazon—over six feet tall! She had very large bazooms and long curly hair. A real knock out.

We ended up at some hangout for other of her ilk, downtown. What a time. All the girls were talking about their latest boob job and having to have their hormones adjusted. From what I gathered, it is bloody expensive.

She told me that there was a very famous male ballet dancer who, when coming to town, would call for her in a limousine to take her back to some ritzy hotel. I guess they had sex. I didn't ask her if she was a "working girl" at the time.

Ellen only dates men. Bloody hell, she is a woman all the way. I think she had the whole operation thing—upper and lower. You'd swear to god that she was a woman. She has a vagina and everything!

EVENING OF SONG

We have one night a week where we can enjoy music. Oh my god, it's bloody painful. Last week, we had a fucking banjo player. He managed to play spoons and the harmonica and punched away at a bass foot pedal all at the same bloody time. This guy played songs that were on the 1901 hit parade. Have *you* ever heard "I'm a daddy / I'm a daddy today/ I'm a daddy / He weighs ten pounds they say"?

Some old hag requested "The Biggest Aspidistra in the World." I'm so sick of shit like "Que Sera, Sera," "Tit Willow," and "Roll Out the Barrel." By this time, everyone is really into it, screeching and clapping. I wish I was anywhere but there.

One night, we had the Singing Duet of Linda and Giles, having just returned straight from LA after a successful tour. She was a brassy, lusty, anorexic bitch. I figure she'd had implants (triple D) with a face-lift so tight that she looked like a cross between Charlie Chan and Barbie. It must have been a successful concert all right. What in the hell were they doing here at a piss-ass place like the Gulag?

The old farts here really enjoyed watching Linda. Especially when Linda bends over the old men and her tits just about fall out of her goddamned dress!

I tell ya. It doesn't matter how old these men are—they are all a bunch of pervs!

EVENING WITH CLAUDE
(pronounced *Clode*. S'il vous plaît!)

I've been waiting for this for a hell of a long time. He scares the shit out of everyone else here. Bloody hell! All the old ladies are intimidated by him. He is six foot five. With his chef's hat, he is about seven feet tall. He reminds me of the Friendly Giant except he ain't friendly.

Why do they always wear the top button open, and no matter what country they are in, they wear those bloody ugly gray-and-white checked pants! I think it's about time to change the style.

There were a lot of people present at the meeting. First of all, chefs are known to present a fucking strong presence. In the kitchen, there can be only one boss. If you watch Gordon Ramsey, you can get a general idea of what it is like in the kitchen when it gets busy. When I was a chef—did I mention that I owned a restaurant?—I had a potato thrown at me once. Don't ever criticize the boss. The meeting went like this: I thought I should be first up because a good attack spells a good defense in my books!

My first point was: "I suggest you take a damn refresher course!" The look in his eyes was deadly. It read, "Why, you old bitch, I'm gonna get cha."

"Just try, you stupid bastard."

My next complaint was: "You can't cook a good steak worth a damn!"

I thought he was going to have a stroke right there and then.

My last dig was: "Are those soggy, limp, tasteless lumps s'posed to be cabbage rolls we had the other night?"

He had enough. I almost felt sorry for the asshole but not quite. I thought I had better not say any more.

FISHING WITH TOM AT PENDER HARBOR

After I got over the shock of finding out that our yacht was a 1960's fourteen-foot fiberglass outboard with no draught piece of shit I figured, well, I gotta suck it up. Since I tied the knot, I found out that he had lied about everything. He had no money, no house, no car, and an ex-wife who was always hounding him. *What did I get myself into?* was my mantra.

I had married a "secondhand Tom"! He never bought anything new. Well, I guess so. He had no fucking money, that's why! I have been trying to understand why in the hell I would marry the little creep after twenty-two years of being alone. He was lousy in bed, as well. I think I was bloody crazy in the head!

Anyhow, that is not what I'm writing about. The first time we went out to fish, it was most embarrassing. After we gassed up the boat, off we went. The first thing he did was pull out his captain's hat. The bastard was going to put the bloody thing on. Try to imagine this—we were surrounded by beautiful yachts owned by millionaires. All I could think was *"Bloody hell! What are we doing?"* My new husband stood at the prow of our yacht, wearing his captain's hat and gave the salute. You'd think he was fucking Lord Nelson saluting his armada or something. All I could do was to slink down so they didn't see me.

The farther we got from shore, the more I started entertaining the thought of getting rid of the little bastard! No one would know . . . or would they? I know they always think of the grieving widow first, so I started thinking of other ways. I know! A slow poisoning, maybe? Well, maybe not now. Later!

PS: Bloody hell! The boat was bobbing up and down so bad that I started to puke. The "'Captain'" had to head for shore. We didn't catch one frigging salmon.

GETTING USED TO THINGS

I'll never forget my first morning. Hey, I'm really here. I felt like puking, that's what. For a minute, I didn't know where I was. *Oh bugger! I'm in the Gulag. I hope they're ready for me. Come on, get up. Carpe diem, atta girl.*

I managed to go down to the dining room and partake of the continental brekkie. What a bunch of yahoos. I hated it. The tea tastes like grass. I should be smoking it instead.

I think I don't like it here either. I'll have to tell my daughter I want to leave. To where? She sure in the hell didn't offer to take me in. She's a rotten kid, and she likes to make my life miserable. At first, I really bitched about things to anyone who would listen. I think my daughters were pretty glad to get rid of me.

They accuse me of being a whiner. My god, I wouldn't be happy unless I was complaining about something, and I'm not about to stop now.

I've begun to realize that "what's for supper?" and "when did my bowels move last?" are the major concerns everyone has around here. I buy twenty-four rolls of ass wipe at a time myself. It's probably all the fruit they feed us. One day, I was sitting on the crapper when a large picture fell off the wall above the toilet and hit me on my beak. I've never ever heard of that before. I sported two black eyes for months after that.

There are some assholes who like to pick their damn nose, on a regular basis, in our classy sitting room on my favorite chair, ugh. They wipe the said "issue" on the arms and side of their chairs. I went to the front desk and complained. She answered that the home could supply tissues, but some cheapskate would probably take the box back to their room anyway. Nose picking must be a man thing. He's not the only one. There're two others. I wonder if their poor wives knew this before they popped off.

I hear there are "light fingers" in here. If they steal Kleenex, god knows what else. There's one sweetheart who thinks she is some sex bomb or something. She has a huge set of breasts and always pushes them out when the men shuffle by in their walkers.

Sometimes I feel that I don't fit in.

GONE TO THE DOGS

I have to laugh like hell when I'm in Australia. I'll be whizzing along the highway with my daughter when she will yell out, "Mom, look, there's another one!" That being a little truck with a giant dog sitting on top. A sign says Dunk a Dog. They are mobile beauty salons for cats and dogs. Some of them offer Hydrobaths, blow-drys, and the works. Yeah, they have them over here too, but you don't expect it in Australia because in Australia the blokes are so macho. Take a gander at some other monikers that are advertised:

Fairy Tails Doggy Day Care
Whaggin Wheels . . . small or tall . . . we wash them all!
Wash and Polish
Dainty Dog
Shampooch
Snips and Clips
Dogs Done Up
Looking Foxy
Bow Wow Meow
Flea Busters
Puss 'N' Woof
Yoggie Doggie
Dog Gone Beautiful
Pimp My Pup

My daughter had a pooch, and everyone loved that dog—especially Jack. The dog had his own beanbag bed, and when it was bedtime, Jack would pull the bloody dog on his bag into the bedroom. It was a real fucking production. I think the bastard loved that dog more than my daughter! That stupid bugger (meaning son-in-law) insisted on giving the pooch chicken bones for supper after my daughter warned him not to! Twice that poor dog had to have a laparotomy to remove bones caught up in his bowels. I never could figure that guy out.

PS: Aussie men are always right. I think they are all dickheads, myself!

BEING SERVED!

The following story is one of my epics. My daughter told me this one.

You can see that Jack is not one of my favorites. For many farting years, I've tried to convince her to leave the bastard. Being the good mother that I am, I couldn't keep my bloody mouth shut!

Why in the hell was she over there in the first place? Her dream was to go to Bondi Beach and meet a blond Greek Adonis, or some shit, and marry the bastard. And that is what she did. Oh my! Well, it didn't take too long for her to find out that she had married an overbearing, stupid, know-it-all dickhead.

Kids came, one after the other, so she really was stuck over there. It took the poor girl all of about twenty-four years to make the split. The following incident was one of a few times she tried to make a run for the hills.

Here's what happened. About a few years into her 'captivity', she finally decided to serve Jack separation papers. It was around Xmas. She told her lawyer that they weren't supposed to do anything until after the New Year. This was because, being the dutiful daughter-in-law, she was hosting the family dinner on Xmas day.

The grog was really flowing and everyone was bloody loving everyone else. But the truth was my daughter disliked the in-laws, the in-laws disliked the daughter-in-law, and Jack was wishing his folks would quit turning on the damn dishwasher.

Then it happened. The doorbell rang, Jack answered it, and a wizened-up old toad was standing with an envelope in his hand. He said, "Are you Mr. Jack Glove?"

"Yeah, what can I do for you?"

"This is for you," the little man said and shoved the said missive into poor Jack's hand.

Oh, I wish I had been there to see the fireworks!

There was a bellow from the hall. She said it sounded like a bull moose in heat or something similar. The shit hit the fan. Jack was screaming at my daughter. She ran into the bedroom and locked the damn door. The old man was yelling at Jack to sue the bitch, and Nannie was crying and saying, "I always told you this would happen, son. Now she is going to get all your money."

A fine time was had by all.

IDA AND LUCILLE

Ida and Lucille are two Yiddish sisters who live here. They're bloody crazy. They are part of the walker brigade. Ida never goes anywhere without her sister, Lucille. They bang down the hall and you bloody well get out of their way if you don't like your shins banged. They played in a Klezmer band when they were younger. They visit the local liquor outlet twice a week to get their booze. Shit! They must drink a lot.

Here's how it goes:

> IDA. Vare are dose denn perogies you were talking about?
>
> LUCILLE: I'm tellink you, Ida, for the hundredth time, nut today, liebchen.
>
> IDA: I tell you true, I dun't like the fud in dis here place, Lucille!
>
> LUCILLE. Velll, too bad. Shot up already!

Scene in dining room again.

> LUCILLE: Vere are your tith, Ida?
>
> IDA: I dunt know!
>
> LUCILLE: For where dit you poot them dis time?

IDA: I vent svimmink, Lucille. I tink dere in the trep.

LUCILLE: Mein gott! Better yu tek dem out bifore.

IDA: Lucille, yu tink I'm crasey? I dunt vant Hymie Newman to see me, dats vy.

Now that's two crazy sisters. Sometimes I want to trip the bitches when they pass me in the hall!

IMMIGRATION

Holy shit! By the time I got through immigration, I needed a stiff drink. Obviously, the bastards don't want me there. The officer was the dykiest looking broad I'd ever seen. They sure make 'em, well . . . like brick shit houses in tornado weather. First of all, she had a bloody five o'clock shadow. I wasn't sure whether she was a tranny who didn't have time to shave, or she was a "she" who had a really severe hormone problem. Either way, she bloody well didn't intimidate this ugly old hag!

"And what is the purpose of your visit?" Etc., etc.

"I'm coming to visit my daughter and to attend the World Fetish convention."

I wasn't really, but I thought I would be a smart-ass and throw that into the mix. How did I know there really was a fetish convention being held in Sydney the next month? I sure hope that little lie doesn't surface to haunt the old hag.

Well finally, the Amazon stamped my passport, and I was on my bloody way, rejoicing.

I've always wondered why all the trucks except the long-distance ones, which can be a thousand feet long by the way, seem to be so damn small in Australia. They resemble Tinkertoys. Another thing is how crazy everyone drives. In other words, they're very shitty drivers.

My daughter who lives here was indisposed, so I had to grab a taxi. I was so mad at her. She and I had a dustup just before I left Canada. I told her that I'd get somewhere to stay instead of staying with her. She was probably happy about that.

I wonder how my Gulagers are doing without me back at the retirement home. Gulagers are a group of like-thinking oldies who support me at my retirement home. It's like a farting sorority. There better not be any funny stuff goin' on while I'm here. You know, like a takeover or something!

MEN ARE THE BOSS IN AUSTRALIA

Well, women's rights *are* fucked up here. Like I said before, sometimes I think I'm in India. Why is it that the first bloody thing people say when you tell them Australia is your destination is, "Oh my god, the men there are so bloody full of themselves"? My grandmother always said, "Where there's smoke, there's a fucking fire going on."

As you know, the ugly old hag is not easily insulted. Mainly because I am usually the insulter, not the insultee. Let me tell you a story. Now, I'm not above a Foster or two, so one day I decided to go into a bar for a brewski. It was a farting hot day and I was sweating like a racehorse. There was me, the bartender, and one bloke sitting at the other end of the very long, brass railed, curved bar. I thought I was in a movie or something. Anyways, the bartender walked over to me and asked me what I wanted. I said I would take a schooner of Foster. He said sure and put it in front of me. He then returned to the asshole at the far end of the bar.

I had an accident and knocked the damn glass over. The bloody bartender saw this happen but didn't make a move. I said, "Yoo-hoo, I need another glass of beer, if you don't mind."

He yelled over, "Yeah, I do mind." And that was it.

I said, "You fucking Aussie bastard. I want another beer."

He said, "Careful, lady, or you are going to be thrown out of here on your ass."

I wasn't sure whether it was because of my gender or because they thought I was an American!

Bloody hell! The next thing I know, I was thrown in jail. They charged me with disorderly conduct and disturbing the peace. My son-in-law had to come and get me out.

My daughter said, "Mom, I told you before, you are in Australia!"

I said, "I don't give a shit. They can throw me in jail all they want. No bloody, stupid, ignorant Aussie is going to break *my* spirit!"

I was in the dog house for a few days after *this* episode.

MOTHER'S DAY OR THE EPISODE OF THE PISS MATS DOWN-UNDER

This is a story told to me by my daughter. It was fucking Mother's Day! Oh, woe is me. My poor girl. That is the bloody day when every woman wants to feel loved and bloody appreciated. I guess this wasn't the day for her. Her beloved fucking, stupid in-laws happened to be visiting . . . again! This resulted in Jack being in a foul mood because he knew that the old folks were eating four times a day again. And that meant him and his folks getting up at the crack of dawn. The damned dishwasher being on all day and night again sometimes because the friggin' wash cycle took all of four hours. Jack had just replaced the last one the previous week.

My daughter had an understanding that, when they were there, she hated them a lot, and it was up to **him** to look after the little "seagulls" himself. That sounded only fair.

When it came time for the gift giving, it was memorable. The old folks gave my daughter a lovely steamer to wash the floors. My daughter started crying. Hell, I don't know why. She kinda took offense. But it was what Jack gave her that finished everything.

He proudly presented her with a set of piss mats for their three bathrooms. Now, they are very popular in Australia. Maybe it is because the fucking men have trouble aiming their little pizzle at the bowl and piss all over the floor? He stated that he had made sure they wouldn't clash with the color of the bathrooms. How bloody thoughtful of him.

My daughter ran crying into her bedroom. Jack was scratching his head in surprise.

PS: My god, that man's dense!

THE UGLY OLD HAG'S VERSION OF AUSSIE MEN

Now, what better topic to start the ball rolling than giving my views on some, not all, of the fucking Australian men. These "somes" have a bloody bad name! And I am going to tell you why.

They are bossy, overbearing, egotistical shitheads. According to them, Australia is the only place to live. There is no other place on earth that even comes close to their place of birth. Bloody hell! When I was there, I thought I was in India. In their distorted minds, the woman comes second. Actually, their fucking mates seem to come first before wife and home.

They are homophobes. According to them, it is a fate worse than death. "You are a bloody fag," is their favorite expression used against their son when the poor little shit does something wrong.

Are there no gays in all of Australia? I bloody well bet there is! Let's put it this way—if I were one, I would immigrate to a more accepting country.

Shit! I was always in trouble when I went down under.

"You've done it again," my daughter yelled at me.

"Well, what did I do this time?"

The answer was always, "You said this," or "You said that."

I kinda feel that my daughter who lives in Australia is going to dislike this book. Well, to put it plainly, I'm going to get into a shitload of trouble because of it.

PS: I hope I am still talking to her after everything!

MYSTERY TRIP AT THE GULAG

Oh my god! Everyone is yakking about the destination of the mystery tour. I don't give a fuck! Just get me out of here for a while. Seems to me we went to Mountain View for the last mystery trip. The Park used to be the favorite place to drive with your sex-thirsty, always-thinking-about-"it" boyfriend. My date for high school graduation drove to the Hollow Tree that night and tried unsuccessfully I wondered what happened to the monkeys. They got rid of them about fifty years back, for god's sake! I've always hated them. Who wants to see them swinging on the trees with their little posteriors staring at you in the face? It's ugly.

On the way back to the retirement home, we stopped in Chinatown to grab come Chinese food. There was one of those lazy Susans in the middle of the table. Someone kept twirling it around just as I was going to grab something. When I managed to turn it back to me, everything I liked was gone!

During all this, we could hear the chef hacking and spitting in the back. Shit! I read somewhere that it is a custom over in China. I felt like vomiting every time he let one go! I wonder if he washes his hands after taking a leak.

I was glad to get back. I don't think I'm going to take another chance going on a mystery trip again. I feel the need of a toke after *that* excursion!

I think it would have been better if some of my Gulagers came along. It's always nice to have some backup.

MY ANDROID

Jeez! I got myself an android cell phone... It was so complicated that I couldn't figure out how to turn the damn thing on. I spent all of the first morning talking to the troubleshooting department.

"Hello, please help me," I whined to the operator in the troubleshooting department.

"Well, ma'am, that is why I'm here," int...

...old man who fucking brags about everything. He took his lady friend on twenty-seven cruises. How bloody boring is that? He's got the biggest teeth I have ever seen in a human being. What's there to do around the ship after you've been on that many cruises?

I think he's got lots of money though. But I think he's kinda tight with it. He's another idiot who talks about his staff of three hundred and blah, blah, blah. Poor guy must have the beginning of dementia.

He repeats himself at least four times in one conversation. The trouble is these jerks all look normal until you have to sit with the buggers for any length of time.

Anyways, everyone is bloody hard of hearing in this place so you get used to repeating yourself three of four times.

Anyways, he carries an Android with him, but I've never seen him get one damn call!

SIGNING MY LIFE AWAY

I can't believe that I am sitting here with my daughter at the front desk of the fucking Gulag, waiting for whoever is coming to talk to me about living here. They have no idea what they are taking on.

Suddenly, she arrived in all her glory. A size zero, for god's sake. Her six-inch stiletto heels clicked on the slate floors. She was obviously a transplanted California girl all right. What the hell

a long body. All my pets seem to exhibit neurotic habits after a while. How's this one? She has a favorite titty that she sucks on when she gets upset. It's triple the size of the other ones. I'm very happy for her. Some of us have to resort to drinking.

Hey, I got hold of a pot cookie the other day. Marmie loved it! My dog Trudie Lou, who has since moved on, had to be put on Valium. I think I should have gone on it instead.

Then we went on the big tour. This place has more features than a cruise ship. Dum-de-dum-dum. They were playing Zamfir on the sound system. How about some rock?

I asked the stupidest question. "Do you have a swimming pool?"

She answered, very tactfully and emphatically, "No."

After, I realized I was a real wanker and that that was a very stupid question. There was no chance in hell to have a pool in a place like this. There was sure to be a wrinkly old body floating on the goddamned water, probably on a regular basis.

Some seniors will do anything to stay young! I don't know why because a lot of them have congestive heart failure and other stuff. I think my daughters are afraid I am going to embarrass them. I have two—one here and one down under. Now, come on. I know my daughter from Australia is damned glad I live here and she lives there.

This ugly old hag marches to her own drum. At this stage of life, she says anything at any time and usually does. I take it that it could be a cause for uneasiness out in public, wondering what's going to come out of her mouth. Have I always been that way? No. I don't know what happened to me. It may have been from a sort of post post post menopause resulting in cranky old hag syndrome.

PARTY TIME ON A CATAMARAN

What a shitting fiasco that turned out to be. Jack's employer puts a party on a catamaran every year for his employers. I happened to be visiting, my daughter in Australia. We were bused to the dock at Sydney Harbour. On the way, I got hammered!! There was a huge barrel of ice-cold Fosters and Tooheys beer in the aisle right beside my seat. I thought I had died and gone to heaven! I've been told by my daughter

Nobody makes my daughter cry.

She has always been kinda on the chunky side. I questioned her, and she said that horrible girl (my daughter doesn't swear) called her a big, fat tart. That was it. Battle stations are called for. I watched this ugly fucker go into the bathroom. My daughter knew what I was going to do and she said, "Mom! Don't do it!" The bitch was going down. I was like a hornet in a bottle!

Next thing, I was in the bathroom waiting for this dame to come out of the stall. When she did, she looked at me and said, "Yeah?"

I said, "You're a fucking bitch. What planet did *you* come off of?"

She ran out of the bathroom, bawling her bloody eyes out.

Next thing I know, I saw her whining to her husband and then they took off. The party was over for her and us.

I have always wondered what happened between the boss and my son-in-law. I never did find out. Hell, I didn't want to know anyway.

PS: One thing about Aussies is that everything is grander and better than any one else in the entire world. What's so hot about the Opera House anyway? Vancouver has a building with fucking sails and stuff, too.

CHRISTMAS WITH TOM AND FAMILIES

The whole damn family from Australia was out to visit my second husband and me at our home. It was our very first (and only) Xmas. At the time, my daughter had only one kid who had a history of wandering off, so I was watching her like a hawk. I was also having my other daughter and her husband, but they didn't have any kids yet. He's a policeman. I sure didn't want any shit to go down during his visit.

girls? You all know the how important "FP" is? I think Don figured he had died and gone to heaven when marrying me because I was one horny bitch. Now, when I think of it, he seemed to be the only one having a bloody orgasm during sex.

Anyways, Mr. Wheelchair Guy brought his girlfriend to the dinner.

Others present were Tom's first wife, who was a RN. She had one fucking leg missing! Lastly, my auntie Doreen was present, or should I say, she appeared to be present. She was all of eighty-five. I think she had advanced Alzheimer's, so she really wasn't aware of what was going on.

Everything seemed to be going well. Just as I was cutting the turkey, someone said, "You better go to your auntie. I think she is in trouble." That was a frigging understatement. She'd shit all over herself. I grabbed her under the arms, one of the guys took her legs and carried her to the bathroom, and we threw the bag into the bathtub. I felt like throttling the woman. In the meantime, everyone was waiting for me. During this fucking fracas, my paraplegic stepson was groping his girlfriend like mad. Holy shit, she was sitting right on his bloody face!

Why do these things happen to me? My daughter from Australia is a little straitlaced. How that happened, I'll never know. She sure doesn't have my genes! All I know was, by the look on her face, she wanted out of there. Jack kept shaking his head from side to side. I guess he had never experienced anything similar to this in Australia.

Somehow or other, we ended having our supper. Everyone and I got quite drunk that night. It ended up being a lot of fun, after I put Auntie to bed.

PS: I divorced Don after fourteen months of hell

TO DRIVE OR NOT TO DRIVE, THAT IS THE QUESTION

I was a bad girl, a very bad girl. Two weeks ago, I scraped someone's farting bumper while I was backing out of a parking lot. I got out of my car and examined the other guy's bumper. Shit! It was a brand new Audi. Just a little paint removed. I looked around and buggered off.

I figured it had been done to me lots of times. Two weeks later, I got a call from the front desk telling me, "There is a ...

... getting out of my car and snooping around the rear end of the Audi. Then it showed me driving off, like a bat out of hell, away from the damn scene of the crime.

To make a long story short, I pleaded guilty and said I was really sorry that I did such a stupid thing. The bastard took my license away. Well, at least I don't have a criminal record.

I think us seniors are the worst drivers around. How come some of my friends here still have their licenses and they only have one eye that works, or they have macular degeneration, or they shake so bad they have trouble holding on to the steering wheel?

Get this, I was in the backseat of a car driven by a fellow resident. We were going to a show. That was a ride out of hell, one I'll never forget. She was pulling out without thinking. We just about had two near rear-ends, and I was in the backseat! A cop pulled us over and read the damn riot act to her.

Going home, she realized that her hazard lights were on. She ended up punching every button on the dashboard and, while trying to find the right bloody button to turn them off, ended up turning the front and rear washers on. My friend, who was sitting in the passenger seat, was scrambling to find out where the damn instructions for hazard lights were in the manual. Honest to god, I thought I was in a Lucille Ball movie.

I hate not driving but prefer to stay out of jail. Hey! I'm the first to admit that I was a fucking menace on the road. They got the old bitch off the road, didn't they?

RECREATION AROUND THE GULAG

It's about time Canada legalized marijuana. My first experience was a brownie a few months ago. It was . . . well, nothing. I waited all evening, hoping for a fucking high, and nothing happened. I finally went to bed and had the best sleep of my life. In the morning, I got up and was staggering all over the damn place. It was bloody delayed action, that's what it was!

This place has happy hour three times a week. That's when the old gals let 'er rip. Shit, some of those old broads can really put the booze away. Triple martinis are the drink of the night. Enid, the Laplander, can really pound them back. My god, here I thought she was religious. I am thinking I should interview her to join us Gulagers. I think it would do her a world of good. Bring her out of herself.

STAYING WITH THE IN-LAWS (AUSTRALIA)

The very first time I stayed overnight at my daughter's in-laws was an experience I'll never fucking forget. Now, my daughter warned me ahead about what it would be like. It was like hell!

After supper, we all went to the living room to visit with one another. We sat and didn't say a bloody word to one another for the first five minutes. The old folks sure in the hell aren't the easiest people to make conversation. The rug made me want to puke. No wonder . . . It *is* the color of puke!

No one said anything, so the old fart turned on his thirteen inch black-and-white TV. Shit! I have a sixty-four inch Smart Samsung waiting for me back home. All they had were two news channels and the third was showing *The Lawrence Welk Show*. They believed that to watch TV, you had to have the room pitch black, so when I had to get up, I couldn't see where I was going and kept banging my fucking shins on everything.

At nine o'clock, we had to retire for the night. Who goes to bed at that time? We did, that's who!

Upstairs we went. My daughter was crabbing at Jack about his mom and dad for not having a proper bed for them. All they had was a lumpy old mattress on the floor. Evidently, the old folks are millionaires. I had a room to myself but the bed was shitting uncomfortable. I could feel the springs digging into my back all miserable night. It was like the Spanish Inquisition!

I had to get up during the night and had no clue where the damn shitter was. The light in the bedside table was burnt out, and I really had to go! I felt for the light in the hall, but every time I flicked it on, Old Fart Face yelled out, "Turn the lights out!" I did it deliberately three of four times, just to make the little troll mad.

On the way back, I accidentally wandered into their bedroom. I proceeded to climb into bed with them. The old bugger let out a bellow, and I soon exited the room. Hey, they probably thought the old hag was in there for some fun. Maybe they were expecting a threesome?

PS: We were told the next morning that we would all go for a walk around the neighborhood. I could hardly wait.

STUFF AND CLIQUES

I don't believe in cliques. Weak people like to join them because they need a mob to back 'em up. Not me! All the gurus say you have to love yourself. I'm doing it. Feels good, and I'm not changing.

I've said before that the dining room is a minefield. I like to go down there and explode the bastards. I'm here to break up cliques. Some of the old-timers sit in the same damn seats every day. Of course, they are the best in the house. You can have a skookum view of the goings-on. I hate watching these old geezers park their hoary old asses every day on these chairs. The other day, I walked over to one of these tables and plunked my ass down on one of them

"You can't sit there," they said.

"Well, I don't see your name on the back of the chair, so I ain't moving. What do ya think of that?" I enjoyed my lunch immensely.

My dad always said, "Dolly, a faint heart never won a fair lady." I think that's why this ugly old bag turned out so well. I'm confident and smart.

I was asked to write something for the local monthly magazine. I did great for a while. Well, I got tired of being nice, which isn't my natural state, so I happened to mention there were bloody misogynists and abused women here at the Gulag! What in the hell is wrong with that? Administration censored me. Narrow-minded bastards!

I'm getting a little following of fellow Gulagers around here. Holy shit, I'm going to have to start interviewing candidates. They are all women that are showing interest. That's because men are such pussies!

THE ACCENT

I have yet to meet an Aussie who can't tell a good joke. Jack, my esteemed son-in-law, is one of them. Shit, he can have us rolling in the aisles. It could be their accent. They say we have an accent. I can't understand a word *they* say. Jack used to roll his eyes (that made the two of us) when either of us said anything. It got to the point that I was going to hire a frigging interpreter. It was that bad!

Aussies are bloody loud. One time I was sitting at a table next to a group of girls, and they were so loud that I couldn't hear the music from a band that was playing. I'm going to get me some fucking earplugs. That ought to do it.

I got myself in real trouble with Jack once. His best mate was over having a cuppa one day. I thought the guy said something like "You should come over to my place for a piece . . ." and the rest was kinda mumbling. Did I get my fucking knickers in a knot over that one! No wonder I couldn't understand him. The jerk had no teeth. I found out, after the guy left, that he was asking me over for a piece of his wife's pie.

I found out quickly that Aussies don't like Americans. Personally, I think it hits too close to home. When you don't sound like an Aussie, they think right away you must be a Yankee. They can be damn rude if they smell USA on you.

This is what I figure. Aussies want your business, but they don't want you moving in. Shit, they make the landed immigrant visa fee astronomical. A few years ago, I asked an immigration lawyer why the visa was so expensive, and he said, "We don't want you here, that's why!"

THE CHOIR AT THE GULAG

Oh my god! I figured, since I had almost made my debut when I was a young girl, I should share my expertise, ya know what I mean? It was a *capital disaster*. The girls didn't want my expertise, not one farting bit. Right away, I knew I had to take control of this mess.

I said, "There has to be one captain of the ship, and that is me."

Wrong . . . again.

I said, "Why in the hell are you sitting with your backs to me?"

I had to stare at their ugly, fat asses instead of their faces. I asked them if they realized that their voices came of their bloody mouths and not their anuses.

In whiny voices, they said, "Well, the other lady liked us to sit that way."

I soon straightened those bitches out. Made them sit in a semicircle facing me, grumbling all the way.

"Okay, let's take a gander at your music," I said. "'It Willow' or 'Roll Out The Barrel' has to go! Shit, you're not dead yet. We're going to change that."

I had them sing for me, which they did willingly.

Well, it was bloody awful. They sounded like a bunch of cats in heat.

By this time, if looks could kill, I would have been struck down immediately. I could see that there was no hope for these songbirds. And there sure as hell no hope for me either.

I quit my position. Never went back. Shit, I have other fields to conquer.

THE IN-LAWS IN AUSTRALIA (AGAIN) OR THE DISHWASHER EPISODE

Don't know where to bloody start. My daughter has a set of in-laws that defy description. Here in Canada, we don't have anything like them. They are fucking unique. And rich.

They hate me! They think I am uncouth and crass. They're probably right. They are both in their nineties and still drive. They don't like profanity of any kind, so my daughter is always looking at me as if waiting for the obvious to happen.

When they come to visit my daughter in Southern Australia, it is a living hell. They get up at the crack of dawn and go to the table and sit, waiting for their breakfast to be served, having already set the table. It's five a.m., and they've already made their bed and had their shower.

My daughter hates them. She refuses to wait on them, so Jack has to drag his sorry ass up and make them their breakfast. Of course, they expect oatmeal porridge, ham and eggs, fruit (prunes, of course, for their fucking regularity), and everything else. Then, after eating, they proceed to put the dishes in the dishwasher and turn it on.

Lunch comes. Guess who's sitting at the table waiting for service? The in-laws. My daughter still really hates them. So that means Jack again has to make them lunch. After, they load up the dishwasher and turn it on.

Teatime! There the little folks are sitting at the table, waiting . . .
just waiting . . . again. My daughter really, really hates them. My son-
in-law has been in the kitchen all day, preparing his ten-veggie dinner.

"It better damn well be good," the old fart mumbles under his
breath. My daughter appears so as to make an appearance at the spread.
You could cut the air with a knife. After the meal, they load up the
dishwasher and turn the bloody thing on for the third bloody time.

We're not finished yet! It's time to have a cuppa just before bedtime.
Out comes the round blue tin, and everyone has to have a piece of her
shitty square that the old lady always brings. I have no idea what it is
supposed to taste like. Again, Jack has to get up and serve them. You
can hear him mumbling in the kitchen, "When are the sons of bitches
going home anyway?"

My daughter loves to hear all this. She likes to see Jack suffer. Guess
what? Again the old dishwasher is turned on for the fourth time!

My daughter is laughing all the way. They have gone through at
least three dishwashers in the last three years!

THE SHED INCIDENT

This is a story that's bloody hard to tell.

It was a day that was like any other day here in Australia. Shitty, that's what. My son-in-law was perched on his flaming lawn mower, cutting his vast acreage. Holy shit, that dickhead loves that lawn mower almost as much as himself. Picture this—Jack sitting on the seat of the mower, with his straw hat perched on his huge, pointed head, holding a stubby of 4XXX beer, and a cigarette hanging out of his yap. There is one compensation. At least when he is out there, he's out of my way.

Dickhead was obsessed with the damn dishwasher as were his crazy parents! What is it about that appliance that sends him into a manic phase? Well, it could be because he has to keep replacing it all the time! If his stupid parents—who resemble a couple of eating, pooping, ninety-year-old little senior seagulls and who insist on turning on the dishwasher every time they eat, which is numerous times on a daily basis, by the way—would stop coming around, he would be a much happier son.

When Jack takes a step, the whole bloody house shakes on its foundation. He thumps around the house like he has two large, fat logs as appendages.

Anyways, he decided it was time for his midmorning smoke He hopped off his lawn mower and went into the kitchen. I was in the front bedroom, staying out of the fray, and I heard him bellow out in a distinctive Australian drawl so bad that I used to have to ask my daughter what in the hell he was saying all the time, which annoyed the bastard to no end, "Dammit! You haven't emptied the damn dishwasher yet."

That was it for my daughter. She plunged out of the kitchen toward the shed where her car was parked. She entered the garage by the side door, jumped in her car, gunned it, and backed out. Unfortunately, she was so mad she didn't press the automatic door opener, so she took the garage door with her.

I heard all this and ran out. Jack was hopping up and down, bellowing with anger! My daughter just stood there and laughed. Next thing you know, I'm laughing too. He's such an asshole!

Honestly, I don't think there is anything wrong with her or me. It's him!

THE SWIMMING LESSON AT THE GULAG

Since this bloody place doesn't have a swimming pool, I had to go out of the house. I can't swim worth a shit. When I was six, I almost bit it at the beach in a small town called Moose Jaw. It's got to be Canadian with that name. I'm proud to say that I am a Canuck. We may be a little rough around the edges, but we have just as many assholes as the USA.

So when I booked my first lesson, I went in my drawer and found my bathing suit. I should have tried the damn thing on before I left. Okay, there I am, standing waiting for the instructor. Shit! My cheeks were hanging out, and I had a bad case of camel toe. I thought, *Well, that might work well for me.* Some of the old farts were noticing me. Christ, they must be crazy. But then, they didn't look so good either. Why is it that the old farts like to wear Speedos? I guess they like to show off their junk? I felt like puking. From experience, I think they are all dirty old men.

I kept pulling my bathing suit down, but my damn ass kept popping out. I had enough of this, and I jumped into the water. Too bad I didn't realize it was the deep end, and I panicked. One of the instructors came to my rescue and dragged me down to the shallow end where my fellow Gulagers were waiting.

Have you ever had the feeling that you don't belong? I hated every shitty minute in the pool. I couldn't wait for the lesson to finish. I was so damn anxious to get out of there that I didn't care if my butt cheeks showed or not. I just wanted to bugger off and get back to the Gulag.

I didn't want to see the inside of a pool again . . . ever.

THE TRIP TO NOOSA

For those who don't know where Noosa is, it is on the Sunshine Coast of Queensland. What a paradise for the old hag! I thought I would be lying in the beach with a drink and watching all the young boys in their Speedos run by. Of course, it didn't happen quite that way. I did see Jack, though, in his eeny teeny budgie smuggler! He has a huge beer belly, so he sure wasn't anything I wanted to look at, never mind what was below the belt!

This time, my daughter had one child, a little girl, who was a holy terror! She was always wandering away. She didn't seem to have the separation syndrome like most kids her age. She would just take off, and we never had any fucking idea where the little shit could be. One time she decided to take off at the beach. One minute we were watching the lifeguards do their thing, and then we realized the little bugger had disappeared. We had them announce her on the intercom, but we couldn't find her. Eventually, some guy said there was a little girl in the men's bathroom. It seemed she ended up there because she needed to poo-poo. I told my daughter to just leave her there, as I was sick and tired of looking for the little wretch.

It was about twenty to midnight on New Year's Eve at Noosa, and the three of us were playing cards. Suddenly, my daughter decided to go to the bathroom. She took off. Time passed and it came to be five minutes to the hour, and she bloody well hadn't come back. I thought,

Where is that damn girl anyways? We called and called, but she didn't answer.

Someone with brains, mainly me, thought she may still be in the bathroom. There she was—locked in the toilet. She was a little chunky, as she called herself, and couldn't fit under the door and certainly couldn't clamber over the top. So she had been hollering for us to come and rescue her. Well, we all started to laugh. How fucking ridiculous. Finally, Jack took a good run at the door and rammed it. It flew open, but the poor girl had nowhere to go and it brained her, knocking her out cold. We spent the fucking night in the emergency ward. She hasn't suffered any injuries apart from her usual weird behavior. She takes after me, obviously.

ON THE WAY TO THE WALMART!

Jeez, this is a big trip . . . The Walmart! Ahhh. Larry, the driver, has arrived. What a fucking sweetheart. Loves us old ladies.

The walker brigade has arrived. It takes Larry ten minutes to load up the walkers first, then the old bags. I feel like a real tool. I'm the only one that doesn't have one. After we got rolling, some of the ladies start yapping at him. They are not supposed to yap at Larry. He's driving.

Suddenly, some little old man vomits all over himself, his wife, and the seat. He says he has his empties with him and wants to go to the government liquor place to return them and get some more beer. The bloody bus smells like vomit. It still stunk for a few weeks after. I don't know what the poor bugger ate, but it was bloody awful.

Before we arrived at Walmart, we had a damn flat tire. That was in the middle verse of "Tit Willow," by the way! Larry was struggling with the lugs (he's s'posed to call someone for help. Obviously, he didn't) but that was bloody okay because we were able to finish "Tit Willow" *and* "Roll Out the Barrel."

Through all this, the lady with the big breasts was rubbing herself on the old guy sitting next to her. God only knows what that could lead to! And Morley, the ninety-five-year-old thespian, was reciting "The Lion and the Mouse" in a very loud voice to whoever would fucking listen to him. We were all listening to him! We had to whether we liked to or not. Bloody hell! I hate that poem. It's the only one he knows. I'm going to get me a pair of earplugs!

We lurched to a stop in front of Walmart, and the whole process of unloading everyone happened again.

PS: Like, I still think this would make a hell of a great reality show. I hate going to Walmart! The only trouble is that their rolls of toilet paper are always on sale.

TUB BATH

We don't have a tub in our rooms, just a walk-in shower! Bloody hell! When you shower, you are forced see your wrinkly, baggy self. At least when you have a bath you can sink under the water and pretend it's not you in there.

I'm a Yardley girl. Always have been. So I grabbed my soap and towel and took off. Why is it that everyone seems to be leaving their rooms when I am making my way to the public bathroom, which is two floors up? It's like running the gauntlet! Why, why? Shit, I hate this. No fucking privacy around here. I didn't know where I was going, but I didn't want anyone to know that. Hey, no doubt they couldn't wait to talk about it downstairs. Oh yes, around here, everything is news. By this time, I didn't care whether I really wanted to make this happen or not.

The bathtub was okay. I started to wonder who had a bath last. Could it have been shitass Andy, whose crotch hangs practically down to the floor? He probably pisses around the toilet all the time. I couldn't find anything in the way of farting evidence. They should have piss mats—they're big in Australia. Anyway, I bought a bottle of Dettol to disinfect the damn tub before I stepped into it.

It was heaven. I poured my lavender bath bubbles under the faucet—$4.95 on sale at Walmart, by the way. I felt like a fucking queen. I was in there for about fifteen minutes, and then there was a knock at the door.

"Who is it?" I said.

"It's the care aide."

"What in the hell do *you* want?" I said.

"Well, Bernice on the second floor was worried about you. She said you were lost."

I said, "Do I look lost? I'm having a goddamned bath. Do you mind?"

It ruined the whole experience. Damn that Bernice, anyway.

WE'RE GOING TO DISNEYLAND

This episode occurred one Summer while my daughter and family were out visiting me. Now, I lived in a little white clapboard house. The damn house was, at the most, about four hundred square feet!

I managed to squeeze the two adults and three kids and me in this bloody midget-sized house. There was wall-to-wall people.

My daughter and son-in-law were feuding before they even came over. Staying in this dinky house didn't improve relations. The kids were whining because they wanted to see fucking snow all the time! One of the grandsons kept saying, "I hate your bloody TV. Why don't you get some good programs?"

The little buggers probably wanted to watch porno. I happened to catch the little motherfuckers with their mates in the back bedroom, watching hard-core porno, when I was visiting in Australia one time, The little fuckers begged me not to tell their mom and dad. And being a good Nan, I said, "Sure."

I'll do anything to keep myself in their good graces. Besides, I don't squeal!

Anyhow, as I was saying, my son-in-law decided they wanted to drive down to Disneyland, so my second husband-to-be, Tom, offered his RV. I think they thought it was an eight-wheeler or something.

Let me tell you about this RV. It was fucking pathetic! Tom bought it for a song from the school board. It was one of those ugly yellow ones with the black-and-white-striped back door. The bastard was bloody cheap. Of course, when I was madly in lust for him, I didn't care if he was stupid or poor. By the way, he turned out to be both of those—and more!

Anyways, he fixed it up with a sink, a mini fridge, and a porta potty. The bed was made with two-by-fours, and he bought a cheap piece of foam for a mattress. Holy shit! It was like sleeping on a rack.

Anyways, back to the original story. It had about four thousand miles on the transmission and was burning oil because you could see the bloody thing coming, surrounded by a huge cloud of black smoke.

So there you are. I'll never forget the look on my daughter and son-in-law's faces.

"What the hell is this?" Jack bellowed out.

"Well, this is your fucking RV," I said.

Tom said, "I've even given you my boat with outboard as well."

"You call that a boat?" said Jack.

It was even worse than the RV. This boat was circa 1960 and had no bloody draught.

PS: They went on their trip, and a shitty time was had by everyone. They had three tire blowouts and had to have the radiator and transmission replaced!

YAKETY-YAK

Oh my god! Some more rules! Now that we can't sit anywhere we want to in the dining room (new dictate from above), I had to sit at a table with Mr. Know-It-All (the world revolves around me, so be my captive audience).

Shit! It was hell. His mouth is never at rest. His voice can be heard above everyone else's. It has been embedded in my brain.

Well, the subject of the day was—he has the best doctors; he is always at the front of a list; his car is the best; his furniture is the best. My god, I felt like asking him if his shit was the best! He told me I was a very dirty woman.

That last statement really got me all riled up. The weird thing was that, up to the time he said this remark, I thought I was being a very good girl. After all, I hadn't written anything of a farting inflammatory nature. Just think what he would think when he gets a gander at this essay. Then I really am a dirty woman.

I had had enough! I told him that I was very excited that his life was so perfect, but as far as I was concerned, he was full of shit!

Well, that shut the bastard up. The rest of the dinner was in complete silence, which was a complete relief. He turned fifty shades of red.

I don't think he wants to sit with me—ever again.

MY FIRST VISIT TO AUSTRALIA

I'm talking to my daughter again. I had to stay in a fleabag motel for one night only, and then she came and picked me up. She and her husband live in a real nice house with a swimming pool. It's so bloody hot here that a pool is really necessary. Jack, my son-in-law, always complains about the pool because he has to have their water trucked in. Shit! He has lots of money. Little does he know that my daughter is always topping the pool and taking a bath in their spa tub all the time.

I remember her calling me one time and telling me they had a really bad brawl, and she ended up doing wheelies on his new lawn. I remember saying, "Way to go. That's my girl. Give 'em hell."

He liked to take us to shoot roos in the evening. Poor buggers. Here they are, hopping all over the place, just minding their own damn business, and some bloody Australian idiot is popping a shot at them. The ones I have seen here are about six feet tall. Luckily, Jack hasn't reached the mark and hit one of them yet. They come out at nighttime. There're lots of them lying dead on the side of the road in the morning. I guess some mad driver nails them. Everyone has heavy roos rails mounted on their vacation vehicle. Shit, if you hit one of those giant roos, it could be game over.

Jack has a vegetable garden out the back. He loves cooking. My god, we have at least ten veggies every meal. I told him I really liked Australian tomatoes, and when I got there, there were bloody tomato plants all over the place. He even planted tomatoes amongst the flowers under all the windows. We have tomatoes for breakfast, lunch, and supper. I'm not complaining.

Jack had a beer fridge, and it was stocked up with Corona beer. Eventually, the Beer Nazi—that's what Jack calls my daughter—started cutting me off at *two beers*. I guess I get kinda mouthy when I've had a few. I vaguely remember doing a little bump and grind out on the porch. Hell, I'm on fucking holidays, the nerve of her.

Last week, the in-laws came up to see me. He seems to be a dirty old man. The silly old bugger likes to talk about sex all the time. I caught him looking down my daughter's top the other day. I don't think he's ever had sex!

NEVER FAIL BAKING POWDER BISCUITS

4 tsp baking powder
½ tsp salt
2 cups of flour
1 cup milk
¼ cup shortening

Chill shortening first then cut it up into dry ingredients then add milk.
Important—mix only fifteen times. Put on a floured board and only knead fifteen times.
Roll out on a floured board.
Bake in oven at 425 °F for about ten minutes or until browned.

UGLY HAG'S SPAGHETTI SAUCE

SAUCE
4 cups of tomatoes
1 tin tomato paste (you can add a tin of tomato sauce if you like also)
1 tsp white sugar (or more if desired)
1¼ tsp oregano
Add Tabasco for taste if you like
1 medium bay leaf
1 tsp salt
½ tsp black pepper

First, sauté approximately 2/3 cup of diced onion and 1 garlic clove in a large saucepan. Then add the above ingredients. Simmer for a while.

MEATBALLS
4 slices of white bread (soak in water and squeeze all moisture out)
1 lb ground lean beef
2 eggs
½ cup grated Romano cheese
2 tablespoons parsley
1 garlic clove
1 tsp oregano
1 tsp salt
Pepper

Form the above ingredients into balls and bake in oven at about 350 °F until brown.

Add them into the sauce and simmer.

DELICIOUS CHRISTMAS WHITE FRUIT CAKE

(Must be kept refrigerated)

4 cups blanched light raisins (sultanas)
2 lbs each of red, yellow, and green candied cherries (cut up fine)
1 lb pecans (chopped fine)
8 oz deluxe fruit mix (no peel)

Boil raisins ten minutes to blanch then drain.
Mix all fruit and nuts.
Dredge with some flour from the following recipe.

1½ cup butter
1½ cups white sugar
4 cups flour
1½ tsp baking powder
1 whole carton (1 pint) whipped whipping cream
6 whole eggs
4 tsp lemon extract
1 tsp vanilla

In a large bowl, mix sugar and butter well then use the cake method to add the rest of the ingredients.

Bake 250 °F in tins, which should be lined with greased paper.

Cooking time varies with size of cake tin. Test by using a toothpick in middle of cake.

GOOD DUMPLINGS

1 cup flour
$1^1/_2$ tsp baking powder
1 tsp salt
1 egg beaten
2 tablespoon melted butter
$^1/_3$ cup milk

Mix all ingredients together just enough to blend all.
Spoon large spoonfuls into gravy.
Put lid on and simmer until cooked (about ten minutes).

DAD'S YORKSHIRE PUDDING (1-2-3 METHOD)

1 cup flour
2 cups milk
3 eggs

Mix well and either place dough around meat in pan with grease or put grease or oil in muffin tins and drop dough mixture into oil.
Cook at 425 °F until risen.

PRESSURE COOKER PORCUPINE
MEATBALLS (MEN LOVE 'EM)

500 grams lean ground beef
1 medium diced onion (save some onion to slice onto meatball before putting lid on)
1 slightly beaten egg
Salt and pepper to taste
½ cup rice (raw)
1 large tin tomatoes
½ cup ketchup

Mix above ingredients in a bowl and form balls.
Cut up tomatoes and place in pressure cooker.
Put ketchup into tomatoes and mix well.

Mix rest of ingredients, and form into balls, place into tomato sauce.

Put lid of pressure cooker on. Bring to cooking to full pressure. Turn heat down to medium, to maintain pressure, and cook for ten minutes.

Remove from heat and cool cooker under cold water right away.

TRIED AND TRUE RECIPES FROM THE UGLY OLD HAG BORSCHT (DOUKHOBOR STYLE)

4 cups of stock, preferably beef
4 medium-sized potatoes (diced)
salt to taste
1 tsp white sugar
½ tablespoon butter
1 large tin of tomatoes (diced)
1 medium tin of Hunt's Tomato Sauce
1 small tin tomato paste
1 small cabbage (shredded)
4 medium carrots (diced)
4 medium beets (diced)
4 medium potatoes
Dill weed (preferably fresh or dried)
1 pint Creamo (can use whole milk instead)

Cut up one of the potatoes and boil in the broth. When cooked, mash it and return it to broth.

In the meantime, sauté in a frying pan, the diced tomatoes (leaving the juice for later), about one cup of shredded beets, and about one cup shredded cabbage in the butter.

Then add this mixture, plus the remainder of the tomato juice to the broth and simmer for a few minutes. Add tomato paste, tomato sauce, the rest of the juice of the tomatoes, diced potatoes, diced beets, diced carrots, and more shredded cabbage to broth.

Don't overcook the vegetables.

Simmer the vegetables until just barely cooked. Lastly, add salt to taste. Add the Creamo *slowly* and take off the burner. Lastly, add the dill weed and some more shredded cabbage. Let it sit for a while.

This soup will marinate well and always tastes better the next day. I find that I like to add a little more sugar.
This delicious soup freezes well.

THE UGLY OLD HAG'S SUPER-DUPER MEAT LOAF

$^2/_3$ cup milk
2 eggs
1 tsp salt
¼ tsp pepper
3 slices fresh bread (crumbled)
1 onion chopped
½ cup shredded carrot
1 cup shredded cheddar cheese
1 ½ lbs lean ground beef

¼ cup brown sugar
¼ cup ketchup
1 tsp prepared mustard

Break eggs into a large bowl, beat lightly with fork. Add milk, salt, pepper, and crumbly bread. Beat until bread has disintegrated. Add onions, carrots, cheese, and beef. Mix well. Put into 9x15 loaf pan. Combine brown sugar, ketchup, and mustard. Spread on loaf and bake at 350 °F for one hour.

Let stand for ten minutes then remove from pan.

BAKED BEANS IN PRESSURE COOKER

You'd think you cooked them for hours in a Crock-Pot!)

soak 2 cups of white beans overnight
1 piece of salt pork (not too large)
1 tsp salt
3 tablespoons brown sugar
3 tablespoons molasses
½ tablespoon dry mustard
1 medium onion
3 tablespoons ketchup or you may use chili sauce instead

Put all ingredients in pressure cooker.
Pour enough hot water to cover beans.
Place the lid on cooker.

Heat until the indicator is up then turn to medium heat and cook for
thirty-five minutes.

EPILOGUE

Folks, the author hopes she didn't offend your sensibilities too much. Everyone has different sides to them, and the Ugly Old Hag series showed you one of her sides. She knows she will be getting bad blogs about her book, but at her age of eighty-one years, she really doesn't take much notice of what people say.

Reiterating what she said in the preface of this book, her characters are pure fabrication—a wild flight of her fancy gone to extremes.

Printed in the United States
By Bookmasters